SAGA

Kelly Hamilton

BROADWAY PLAY PUBLISHING INC
224 E 62nd St, NY, NY 10065
www.broadwayplaypub.com
info@broadwayplaypub.com

SAGA
© Copyright 1983 Kelly Hamilton

All rights reserved. This work is fully protected under the copyright laws of the United States of America. No part of this publication may be photocopied, reproduced, stored in a retrieval system, or transmitted, in any form or by any means, electronic, mechanical, recording, or otherwise, without the prior permission of the publisher. Additional copies of this play are available from the publisher.

Written permission is required for live performance of any sort. This includes readings, cuttings, scenes, and excerpts. For amateur and stock performances, please contact Broadway Play Publishing Inc. For all other rights please contact William Morris Endeavor, 11 Madison Ave, NY NY 10010, 212 586-5100.

Cover art by William Sloan, THREE

First edition: August 1983
This edition: October 2017
I S B N: 978-0-88145-012-5

Book design: Marie Donovan
Typeface: Palatino & Baskerville set by BakerSmith Type, NYC

LYRIC THEATER OF NEW YORK
THE PLAYS IN PROGRESS SERIES

THE WORLD PREMIERE PRODUCTION
April 19, 1979

SAGA

Book, Music and Lyrics by Kelly Hamilton
Musical Direction, Vocal Arrangements by Bruce W. Coyle
Choreography by Colleen Heffernan
Set Design by Terrence B. Byrne
Costume Design by Susan Cox
Lighting Design by John Vetere
Produced and Directed by Neal Newman

WANDERING YOUNG MAN:	Stephen Bogardus
THE WEAVERS OF LEGEND:	
1st WEAVER:	Richard Stillman
WEAVER WOMAN:	Megan McPherson
3rd WEAVER:	Paul Canestro
PURITAN GIRL:	Mara Beckerman
COTTON MATHER:	Tony Calabro
THE DEVIL:	Scott Hunt
ANNE HUTCHINSON:	Angelina Reaux
TOWN CRIER:	Jay Aubrey Jones
TAILOR:	David Sloan
TAILOR'S WIFE:	Sharon Talbot
OLDER CHILD:	Stacy Peppell
YOUNGER CHILD:	Ellyn Gale
JENNY:	Karen Longwell
YOUNG SAILOR:	Mark Wolff
TEACHER:	Karen Longwell
DANIEL BOONE:	Daryl Hunt
MIKE FINK:	Tony Calabro
BARBARA ALLEN:	Karen Longwell
GEORGE DONNER:	David Sloan

TAMSON DONNER:	Angelina Reaux
PIONEER WIVES:	Sharon Talbot, Mara Beckerman, Teresa Parente, Deborah MacHale
SETTLER MOTHER:	Tianna Jo Schlitten
SETTLER CHILDREN:	Stacy Peppell, Ellyn Gale
JOHNNY APPLESEED:	Richard Stillman
HOPPIN' JOHN:	Stephen Bogardus
49RS:	Jay Aubrey Jones, Mark Wolff
JULIA BULETTE:	Angelina Reaux
MATRON:	Barbara Porter
EVANGELINE:	Karen Longwell
MINSTRELS:	Jay Aubrey Jones, Daryl Hunt, David Sloan, Mark Wolff
AUCTIONEER:	Tony Calabro
COUSIN SAL:	Karen Longwell
CREOLE WITCH:	Deborah MacHale
CREOLE MYSTICS:	Teresa Parente, Mara Beckerman
MARIE LAVEAU:	Angelina Reaux
JOHN BROWN:	Tony Calabro

STAFF

Production Stage Manager:	G. Michael Trupiano
Assistant Stage Manager:	Sally Hopkinson
Assistant Director:	Jayne Luke
Assistant Choreographer	Dan MacDermott
Assistant Costumer:	Robbynne Archia
Assistant Producer/Casting:	Maximilian St. James
Electrician:	Susan McCafferty
Posters & Flyers	Bruce Lemerise
Publicity:	Doug Cole, Maximillian St. James
House Manager:	Thea de Franchesca
Special Banjo Arrangements:	Richard Stillman
Program:	Karen Siegel

Act One

Scene: The setting is an abstraction. As sparsely and simply as possible, it suggests an open, rural area where something historical or ceremonial might once have taken place. In some indefinable way, an essence of the past seems to hover over the place, as though events of great importance have left an emotional imprint.

At rise: The area is shadowed in the dusk of late summer, and only the faint sound of crickets breaks the silence. HOPPIN' JOHN *enters. He is a restless young man with brooding eyes; and though his dress suggests a timeless quality, there is in his manner something that indicates a man who has spent a good deal of time wandering. At the moment, he is weary, and sits down to check his bearings. He takes out a parchment map, unfolds it, studies it, checks the stars, realizes he is lost. With coming evening, he's not sure whether to stay or move on. A moment of indecision, and at last he gets up to go, when suddenly an eerie theme is heard on violin, as if rising from some unseen source in the shadows.*

The crickets stop, and a hush has fallen. The theme is repeated, and HOPPIN' JOHN *is spellbound, seeming to have recognized and understood the significance of what he is hearing. He sings, softly.*

HOPPIN' JOHN: The weavers of legend are
Weaving tonight,
Weaving tonight,
Some have heard them . . .
Now, I hear them, too . . .

(He takes in his surroundings with new appreciation)

The spinners of fancy are
Spinning tonight . . .
Why not listen awhile . . .
While they do . . .

Lights reveal an area where THREE WEAVERS OF LEGEND *are situated around an imaginary loom. These characters, an old woman* and two old men, suggest ancient storytellers from America's dim past, and have the look of being encrusted with time. As they sing, their choreographic movements suggest abstractions of spinning and weaving.

WEAVERS: The legends we told at
Summer gatherings,
Summer gatherings,
Under the stars;
It seems to me they may fade away,
Unless we tell them today.

In the half-light, a small ensemble of PLAYERS *faintly appear. Their function throughout the play will be to recreate the people, places and events of legend as they unfold. They join the* WEAVERS *in the song.*

WEAVERS and PLAYERS: And, the ballads we sang, at
Autumn's ending,
Autumn's ending,
Around the fire;
It seems to me, when the world grows cold,
They'll be sweeter than lavender,
And much more precious than silver to hold.

HOPPIN' JOHN: *(Moving among the group, expansively)*
Come, gather the bright ballads
And legends for me,
And thread them together
On yesterday's loom;
And weave up a bright tapestry,
Wide as the sea,
In colors of autumn
And summer in bloom . . .

ALL: We'll patch a quilt on
Winter evenings,
Winter evenings,
Patterned and plain,
And it seems to me,
When the earth turns chill,
We'll be patching bright, unmatching
Bits and pieces, still.
Weaving a tapestry, threaded with song,

ACT ONE

Stitched up and patched up
With legends that we were so long gathering,
All a-gone gathering, all summer long.

The PLAYERS *have begun to move, taking on characterization for the evening's first legend. It should be pointed out here that costumes are intended to be balletic and non-specific, with details of place and period suggested through choreography and stylized staging. The overall effect is of images that take shape out of flames and air, shimmering, changing, disappearing, to be quickly replaced by other images.*

HOPPIN' JOHN: *(With growing anticipation)*
The people of legend are
Walking tonight,
Walking tonight,
I can feel them, all around . . .

The PLAYERS *continue to take their places, and* HOPPIN' JOHN *moves in closely to* WEAVER WOMAN, *leaning over her shoulder to view the imaginary tapestry. He speaks apprehensively.*

HOPPIN' JOHN: What scene are you weaving, first?

WEAVER WOMAN: *(Irritated at the interruption, but holding up an imaginary thread)* The thread is grey. Puritan grey.

The PLAYERS *have taken formal positions in the pale dusk. A gentle* PURITAN GIRL *now calls to the group.*

PURITAN GIRL: Come, gather together
For evening song . . .

PURITANS: Alle–Lu
Alle–Lu
Alle–Lu—Jah!

Alle–Lu
Alle–Lu
Alle–Lu—Jah!

WEAVERS *have stitched up the black-clad figure of tall, imposing* COTTON MATHER, *who has taken his position before the congregation.*

WEAVER #1: I think it needs a touch of red!

COTTON MATHER *grows suddenly very agitated as the scene is plunged into scarlet. In shock and horror, he cries out to the congregation.*

COTTON MATHER: I've been told
That the devil is loose! It's
Possible, in Massachusetts
Today!
So everybody, *pray*!

The entire congregation is plunged into fervent prayer. In counterpoint to this, we hear the sprightly tune of a violin. Someone—or something—unseen is dancing through the crowd, and several PURITANS *have looked up from their prayers to take note.* COTTON MATHER *and several* MINISTERS *look on in horror and sing.*

COTTON and MINISTERS: Down, down!
The Devil is a-fiddling
In Salem town,
And the people all begin
To hearken to the music!
Down, down!
The Devil is a-fiddling
In Salem town!

WEAVERS: And they come from Boston,
Lynne, and Beverly!

CONGREGATION: *(As several members are caught up in the dance)*
Down, down!
He plays upon the fiddle
An old country reel,
And the people gather 'round
A-dancin' to the music!
Down, down,
The Devil is a-fiddling
In Salem town!

Several of the congregation become self-appointed judges.

JUDGES: And in the name of sweet religion,
The people will burn
And in the name of sweet religion,
The people will hang,

ACT ONE

And in the name of sweet religion,
The people will die!!!!

WEAVERS *have quickly stitched up the figure of tall, brave* ANNE HUTCHINSON, *dressed in Quaker grey. Drawn by the Devil's music, she is whirled through the dance and thrown before the* JUDGES.

JUDGES: Anne Hutchinson, Quaker in Salem,
Anne Hutchinson, Quaker in Salem,
You shall hang today!
You shall hang today!
You shall hang today!

ANNE HUTCHINSON: *(Defying them all)*
On gallows hill,
There's a twisted tree,
Where a twisted, knotted noose
Is hanging down, down, down for me!

CONGREGATION: Down, down, down!
Down, down, down!
Down, down, down!

ANNE HUTCHINSON: *(Scorning their threats)*
But in the name of my sweet, sweet God,
And in the name of this sweet new land,
I shall not die,
I shall not die,
I will not die, today!

HOPPIN' JOHN and WEAVERS: *(As a Quartet, in canon)*
What became of the people who loved God?
What became of the people who sang His praise?
What became of the people who loved Him,
They're dancing to the devil's music now!

What's become of the power and glory?
What's become of the people who sang His song?
What's become of the people who loved Him?
They're dancing to the devil's sweet violin!

The congregation begins to sing sweet, joyous "Halleluiahs" as the MINISTERS *pull themselves together and begin to drag the accused persons from the crowd.* COTTON MATHER *chants with growing mania.*

COTTON MATHER: To the churches, everybody goes,
From the pulpit, somebody cries,
To the prisons, everybody goes,
On the gallows, everybody dies!

Goody Nurse will hang for a witch,
Goody Proctor hang for a witch,
Mary Dyer hang for a Quaker,
Robert Calef, hang for a Quaker
While the people are singing their
Halleluiahs!

ENSEMBLE: *(With mounting hysteria)*
Down, down
The Devil goes a-jiggin'
Around Salem town,
Everybody, down, down,
To the rhythm of the music!
Down, down, the Devil is a-fiddling,
Down, down, the Devil is a-fiddling,
Down, down, the Devil is a-fiddling,
In Salem town,
In Salem town,
In Salem town!!!

The PURITANS *have been dancing wildly and helplessly to the Devil's song. There exists a 17th Century woodcutting of just such a scene, the depraved dancers having worn their legs to bloody stumps as the Devil continues to fiddle. Such a grotesque effect should be suggested choreographically.*

HOPPIN' JOHN *has shrunken away from the scene, horrified at the nightmare created in the evening's first weaving. The* WEAVERS, *too, have drawn back from their loom, awed by their own power. Quickly, now, they gather new threads, and begin to work silently.*

The scarlet of religious zeal has given way to brooding greens and blues. Through the wake of the chaos, one of the PLAYERS *assumes the attitude of a* TOWN CRIER, *and tolls a mournful bit of news that further concerns* ANNE HUTCHINSON, *who seems to be a token martyr in New England.*

TOWN CRIER: *(Pointing at* ANNE*)* Mother Leeds
Just gave birth to another Devil,

Over in New Jersey now.
With the head of a horse
And the wings of a bat,
And it skirts the pines
And cedar swamps
And it dries the cows
And sours the milk,
As it winds its twisted way
To the sea . . .

Other PLAYERS *have been circling* ANNE, *who has stood unflinching throughout.*

PLAYERS: To the sea . . .
To the sea . . .

They have assumed new characterizations, now, suggesting OLD SALTS *and* SEAWIVES. ONE OF THE LATTER *is bidding* ONE OF THE FORMER *off to sea with a warning.*

SEAWIFE: 'Twere a spectre ship, sighted just off Gloucester.

OLD SALT: *(Nodding. He's heard it all before)* Aye, and 'twere a serpent seen, all coiled on the rocks, just off Marblehead.

SEAWIFE: Mind now, and watch for the Witch of Wellfleet. (ANNE *again)* She's ridin' the tides in the belly of a whale, these days, and I'll thank ye to have a care!

ANNE HUTCHINSON: *(With a disgusted laugh, moving out of the scene)* More superstitions. More tales told by old wives.

SAILOR BOY: 'Twere a phantom seen of a beautiful maiden, watchin' at the shoals. Thrice this week, a' twilight.

As ANNE HUTCHINSON *has exited,* JENNY, *a ghostly young woman in grey has appeared, gazing out to sea.*

OLD SALT: Superstition. I'm sailing with the tide.

The mists roll in, and THREE CHILDREN *begin to sing, as if playing a game in the streets of Mystic or Boston.*

CHILDREN: Seaman's brides and sailor's wives
Count the years by three's and five's.
That's how they spend their days,
That's how they spend their lives.

SEAWIVES *begin softly to chant, as they pace.*

SEAWIVES: Walk and weave . . .

Several of the men have assumed the characterization of SAILORS, *gazing over the prow of a phantom ship. They sing to the women who wait on the shore.*

SAILORS: You walk your windowed rooms,
And weave your nets of twine,
And ever scan the far horizon.
And home to Cape Cod, home to Cape Ann, home to Nantucket
Soon they'll come,
They that go down to the sea in ships,
They that go down to the sea.

JENNY, *the ghostly watcher at the shoals, stands out from among the other women who wait, being younger, prettier, and more filled with hope. She seems to be particularly drawn to one of the young sailors at the prow of the ship.*

Watching from his own area, HOPPIN' JOHN *seems to identify with the aforementioned young sailor. He is very much drawn to the beautiful* JENNY, *and when the* YOUNG SAILOR *sings the following solo, it is almost as if he is articulating* HOPPIN' JOHN's *inner thoughts.*

YOUNG SAILOR: There's a whiteboard cottage
On a low Massachusetts bay,
Where the grey gull drifts,
Ever low upon the shallows.
There my Jenny waits,
With a whale oil lamp lit low,
And she listens to the clock,
And it says, he'll be home tomorrow . . .

JENNY: He'll be home tomorrow . . .

SAILORS: She walks the sandy dunes
That weave beside the shore,
And ever scans the far horizion.
But home to Cape Cod, home to Cape Ann, home to Nantucket
They don't come,

ACT ONE

They that go down to the sea in ships,
They that go down to the sea.

YOUNG SAILOR: It's been many long years
Since I left Massachusetts Bay;
Still the grey gull drifts
Ever low upon the shallows.
And my Jenny waits
With a lamp that has long grown cold,
And she listens to the clock
And the salty winds of sorrow . . .

JENNY: And the winds of sorrow . . .

SAILORS: You walk your widows' walks
And weave your widows' weeds,
And ever scan the far horizon.
But home to Cape Cod, home to Cape Ann, home to Nantucket
They don't come,
They that go down to the sea in ships,
They that go down to the sea
To the sea
To the sea . . .

JENNY *fades from view, and the* OLD SALTS *and* SEAWIVES *move into neutral positions around the stage.* HOPPIN' JOHN *is very much disturbed by the ghostly young girl, and tries to shake away the feelings that have managed to touch him across the chasm of space, time and dimension. He speaks to the* WEAVERS *over melancholy underscoring.*

HOPPIN' JOHN: I don't understand any of this . . .

WEAVER MAN #1: *(Irritated)* Who is this person?

HOPPIN' JOHN: Don't you have any bright colors for that tapestry?

WEAVER MAN #2: Go on home, boy, and don't tamper with the past.

HOPPIN' JOHN: It's *not* the past, not if you're weaving it *now*!

WEAVER MAN #1: Who is this person?

HOPPIN' JOHN: And I *will* tamper with it!

WEAVER WOMAN: The past is a pretty fragile thing to fool around with.

HOPPIN' JOHN: If you can reach back, then so can I.

WEAVER MAN #1: Who *is* this person?

WEAVER MAN #2: Some itinerant malcontent, obviously.

WEAVER MAN #1: Obsessed with the past.

HOPPIN' JOHN: *And* the present, *and* the future!

WEAVER MAN #1: *(With a scornful laugh)* His interests are all-encompassing.

WEAVER WOMAN: *(Kindly)* His interests are genuine.

HOPPIN' JOHN: Back where I come from,
I want to go
Back where it all began . . .
Back where the world was summertime new,
Robin's egg blue, every morning . . .
(He breaks off) Can you weave me into that tapestry?!

WEAVER MAN #1: What, a gangling giraffe like you!

WEAVER MAN #2: Caught up in our delicate loom!

WEAVER MAN #1: No!

HOPPIN' JOHN: Where is it written
That yesterday
Only belongs to some?
There could be a precious part of a dream
And hope for things to come,
Something of value that's waiting
Back where I'm from.

WEAVER MAN #1: *(Unpersuaded)* Cornpone and nonsense!

WEAVER MAN #2: It won't wash, boy.

WEAVER WOMAN: No, I think he has a point . . .

WEAVER MAN #2: She's always been a soft touch for homespun philosophy.

ACT ONE

WEAVER WOMAN: We *could* weave him into the tapestry, you know we could.

WEAVER MAN #2: Well, he's right about one thing, it *is* too dark.

WEAVER WOMAN *has begun to dig into her baskets, and has started threading the loom.*

WEAVER MAN #1: What are you doing?

WEAVER WOMAN: Bright colors, we can weave him in bright colors, and give him lots of character. It would improve the pattern, you can see for yourselves.

WEAVER MAN #1: Now she's an artist.

WEAVER WOMAN: *(Stubbornly)* It will give strength to the tapestry.

WEAVER MAN #2: All right, all right, weave him in—but have done with it, or we'll be here all night!

Lighting suggests that HOPPIN' JOHN *is being transformed as the* WEAVERS *begin to work at the loom.*

HOPPIN' JOHN: Roll back, you rivers,
Fold back, you mountains,
Turn back, you winds
And sweep the dust of time away,
And take me back where I come from
Today!

WEAVER MAN #2: You're in the tapestry, boy—so see that you make yourself useful!

WEAVER WOMAN: Stir up a breeze, set things in motion—!

HOPPIN' JOHN: *(Singing joyously, trying to rouse the sleeping figures in the tapestry)* There's a new country wind
A-comin' up a river,
Blowin' in the canebreak,
And as the wind is changing,
The people follow!
I'm the new country man,
I've got to keep a-moving,

Got to keep a-changing,
Keeping just ahead of
The new country wind,
I can't stop now!

(He looks around him, where the PLAYERS *have remained in stasis. He tries to urge them to life and motion.)*

Men plant roots
And fence in their cottages,
And live one life on one plot of land;
But can't you see, there isn't time to settle,
Only time to expand . . .
Can't you hear it, cross the hills,
From the valleys, farms and mills,
Hey, the new country wind is on the way,
And there's a new country born today.

JENNY, *the ghostly young seawife from the previous scene, now reappears as* BETSY, *a delicately pretty Colonial girl. She is flanked by the* CHILDREN, *and the song she sings to them appears to be partly a game, and partly a lesson.*

BETSY: Thirteen colonies sat by the sea,
And decided that they should be free.
Thirteen reasons for one revolution,
Thirteen daughters of England,
Stitching up a patchwork banner to wave.
And all the red rockets were shot to the heavens,
And all the white stars came falling through,
To land on a field of blue, my love . . .

(She has moved across the stage, and now smiles over her shoulder to HOPPIN' JOHN*)*

For you, my love,
For you.

HOPPIN' JOHN *has been transfixed by* BETSY's *fresh charm, and takes a tentative step after her; but she has moved off with the children. Her presence has touched and inspired him, however, and his voice swells with pride.*

HOPPIN' JOHN: In the bright morning sun,
The new country colors unfurl . . .

ACT ONE

And the new country wind
Sweeps west, through the forests and hills . . .

All around him, the PLAYERS *have been brought back to life, as one by one they are touched by the spirit of the wind. The stage is shot golden with the morning sun, and they begin to sing.*

PLAYERS: Appalachian morning,
Time to begin again;
Appalachian meadows are green to me now,
And how the rivers run with new melting snow.

Appalachian morning,
Time to be born again;
Appalachian summer will come before long,
Be up and on your way, you know where you're bound!

Hello, New Day,
Hello . . . !
Appalachian morning,
I got up late,
But in the foothill meadows,
The sun didn't wait!

Hello, mountain morning,
Hello . . . !
Appalachian mountain morning song,
Appalachian mountain morning song!

HOPPIN' JOHN *has moved in among the ensemble.*

HOPPIN' JOHN: I face the misty mountains,
They are silent,
But they dare me to cross them;
And the trees that weave within them
Are silent,
But their fingers reach to me!

PLAYERS: And in the foothill meadows,
On the lowland rivers,
The winds keep on whispering low
To the white mountains,
Green mountains,
Black mountains, Go!
To the Blue Ridge and the Cumberlands,

Away, away!
Through the red maple,
Black locust, and
White oak and willow . . .
Through sweet gum and slippery elm
Go . . . go!

HOPPIN' JOHN: Bring me men to cross the mountains!
Bring me men to fell the trees and show the way—
And I'll cross the Appalachians today!
Appalachian morning,
Time to believe again!

PLAYERS: Appalachian new world, I'm coming your way;
Appalachian new life, starting today!

HOPPIN' JOHN: Hello, mountain morning
Hello . . . !

PLAYERS: Believe again, begin again, be born again, today!
Hello, mountain morning, hello!
Hello, mountain morning, hello!
Hello, mountain morning, hello!

PIONEER MEN *begin to appear from within the midst of the* PLAYERS, *streaming as if from the mountains to make up what will be the frontier.*

HOPPIN' JOHN: *(Exhilarated)*
Now, The barrier is broken!
Now, let the wide frontier begin!
Now, I need a man to lead these men,
Larger than life,
Someone to lead these men!

PIONEER MEN *have gathered, but they are relatively unseemly characters, and not at all these whom we would have for our heroes.* HOPPIN' JOHN *shakes his head at the bunch, then turns desperately to the* WEAVERS, *who have been watching with interest.*

HOPPIN' JOHN: *(To* WEAVERS*)*
Call out the weavers of legend,
Bring on the makers of myth;
They who spun sagas in Iceland,
They who sang ballads in England,

ACT ONE

Bring them into the tapestry,
We need them here!

(THE WEAVERS *laugh, exasperated with* HOPPIN' JOHN, *who actually seems to be calling upon them to step into, and become part of, their own tapestry)*

Come, all you spinners of fancy
Here, round our fire we need you,
Telling stories and making heroes of men!

Suddenly, his enthusiasm and joy affects them, and the idea grows delightful. So, feigning irritation, but enjoying immensely the sense of participation, they weave themselves into the frontier.

Immediately upon their arrival, HOPPIN' JOHN *pushes a seedy character into their midst. The number grows to a full chorale as the* WEAVERS *begin to transform the mortal man into a* HERO.

PIONEER MEN: Let the weavers of legend make him tall,
Let the weavers of legend make him strong,
Let the weavers of legend make him real;
Let all the weavers make him real,
All the weavers!

WEAVERS: Sing a song of a mountain man,
You're gonna need him to carry you
Over the timbered mountains.
Find him, there with the backwoods boasters,
Down in Kentucky and down into Tennessee!

MEN AND WEAVERS: Hey, mountain man,
Hey, mountain man!
He's gonna (hey!) need a flintlock,
Powderhorn, buckskin, coonskin,
And none too soon,
The people will sing a ballad about him
And call him "Daniel Boone"!

The man has become DANIEL BOONE, *and befitting the name.*

MEN: Let the weavers of legend make him tall,
Let the weavers of legend make him strong,
Let the weavers of legend make him real!

DANIEL BOONE: *(Bellowing over the chorus)* Fresh from the

backwoods, half horse, half alligator, a little touched with the snapping turtle!

MEN: Let all the weavers make him real,
All the weavers!

WEAVERS: *(Choosing another man from the group)*
Sing a song of a keelboat man,
You're gonna need him to ferry you
Over the muddy water;
Find him, king of the ringtailed roarers,
Down Illinois and Missouri and Arkansas way!

MEN AND WEAVERS: Hey, river man,
Hey, river man,
He's gonna (hey!) need a barge
Or a shanty-boat, flatboat, or any boat
The river won't sink,
And the people will sing a ballad about him,
And call him "Mike Fink"!

MEN: Let the weavers of legend make him tall,
Let the weavers of legend make him strong,
Let the weavers of legend make him real!

WEAVERS *have transformed another man into* MIKE FINK.

MIKE FINK: *(Shouting it out over the music)* I'm a Salt River Roarer, a Ring Tailed squealer, a reg'lar screamer from the old Massassip'! *Whoop!*

MEN: Let all the weavers make him real,
All the weavers make him real,
All them weavin' weavers weavin' legends!

MIKE FINK *and* DANIEL BOONE *have squared off, and the number grows into a friendly contest between them. Over music, they out-brag one another.*

DANIEL BOONE: Can wade the Mississippi, leap the Ohio, ride upon a streak of lightening, and slip without a scratch down a honey locust!

MIKE FINK: Can outrun, outjump, outshoot—

DANIEL BOONE: Outbrag!

ACT ONE 17

MIKE FINK: Outdrink, an' outfight, rough 'n' tumble—

DANIEL BOONE: No holts barred!

MIKE FINK: Any man, on both sides the river from Pittsburgh to New Orleans an' back again!

Choreographically, the contest becomes intensely physical: jumping, wrestling, log-rolling, shooting, a totally masculine fantasy into which all of the PIONEER MEN *are drawn. It is playful, rough and wild, and the movement embodies all images of the frontier spirit.*

THE PLAYERS *take up the lyrics again, letting the number build to a rousing finale.*

PLAYERS: And the weavers of legend made 'em tall,
And the weavers of legend made 'em strong,
And the weavers of legend made 'em real!
And all the weavers made 'em real,
All them weavin' weavers weavin' legends!
Hey!
All the weavers made 'em real,
All the weavers made 'em real,
All them weavin' weavers weavin' legends
Hey!

Dusk has fallen, and the men have exhausted themselves. HOPPIN' JOHN *is happy-tired, with the good feeling of having accomplished something.*

THE MEN *all settle down to campfires and the coming night. The sounds of evening birds filter through, and suddenly there is a powerful sense of the expansive loneliness of the frontier.*

HOPPIN' JOHN *is alone by his own campfire. The gentle, random strumming of a guitar now seems to underscore the melancholy that is closing in on him. Something is missing, and his brooding eyes begin to scan the quiet scene around him.*

The haunting theme is heard, and a girl's voice echoes from the night. HOPPIN' JOHN *looks up, and in the distance,* THE GIRL *appears, as though created in his memory. No longer* JENNY *or* BETSY, THE GIRL *is changed, dressed in gingham of pale, moonlight colors, and she grows very beautiful now, made so by* HOPPIN' JOHN'S *need for her.*

HOPPIN' JOHN: *(Softly, wistfully)* Could the weavers of legend Make *her* real . . . ?

WEAVERS: *(Nodding, beginning to bring the girl to life.)*
All around, the campfires burning;
Silver dusk has fallen.
A man spins a dream from loneliness,
And we'll call her . . . "Barbara Allen."

HOPPIN' JOHN: *(Savouring the name)* Barbara Allen . . .

BARBARA ALLEN *comes to life now, and reaches for him, tentatively.*

HOPPIN' JOHN: Barbara Allen . . . will you come West with me?

BARBARA: *(Smiles, gently, reassuring. Slowly, she comes down to him and begins to sing)* Stop now, and rest awhile,
And we'll pretend
It's this journey's end, awhile,
Though I know
You've still awhile to wander.
But stop counting miles awhile,
And maybe we can stand
And count the stars awhile,
Hand in hand, my love.

Let me fill your world with pretty things,
Let me fill your cup from sweetwater springs;
We'll share and settle,
And plough the meadow,
And build a room
Where our first and last are born.

I'll sew you a shirt of linsey-woolsey,
Quilt you a blanket, warm and downy,
And weave pretty baskets, deep and wide,
To carry our love forever,
Wherever you go.
But now, my love, be still awhile,
And let the others chase the winds
On the hill, awhile.
We are free,
To share and settle,
And plough the meadow . . .

There's still awhile
To rest awhile, for just awhile,
My love.

HOPPIN' JOHN: *(Caught up in an incredible new dream)*
I'll build a city on the river
For you, my love,
And we'll call it Saint Louie,
And soon, my love,
We'll see the people gather here,
And watch the people settle here,
And this, too, will be
A part of our dream.

In the city of Saint Louie,
We'll sleep tonight.
So, let the other wagons roll,
For, though I'm bound to follow soon,
First you and I must settle the land.

BARBARA and HOPPIN' JOHN: And now, my love, be still awhile,
And let the others chase the winds
On the hill, awhile.
We are free,
to share and settle,
And plough the meadow.
There's still awhile
To rest awhile, for just awhile,
My love . . .

During the song, the other PIONEER MEN *have slept, as if through a single night.*

The faintest pearl-grey of dawn edges across the prairie, and the MEN *begin stirring, with much murmuring among them that begins to form into words.*

MEN: *(Whispering, so it sounds like the rustle of wind-swept prairie grass)* Keep the frontier moving,
Keep the frontier moving,
Keep the frontier moving on . . .
Get the wagons rolling,
Get the wagons rolling,
Keep the frontier moving on . . .

HOPPIN' JOHN *has fallen asleep in* BARBARA's *lap as she continues gently to caress him. Among the other men, there is packing and suggestions of a wagon train forming choreographically. There begins some awkward confusion among the men.*

MAN #1: Twelve pounds of coffee . . . fifty pounds of bacon. Hey, you call that any way to pack a flour barrel?

MAN #2: Hanged if I know. Do you call that any way to set an axel to rights?

In their confusion, the men begin to turn to one another.

MIKE FINK: Don't ast me, I'm a river man.

DANIEL BOONE: An' don't ast me, I'm a backswoodsman, don't forget it.

MAN #3: Well, we're not going to get west without a little more knowhow, that's for sure . . .

THE WEAVERS OF LEGEND *have been watching with mild interest, and now they step in to take over in the creation of an appropriate new hero.*

WEAVERS: Sing a song of a wagon man,
You're gonna need him to carry you
Over the open prairie.
Find him, there where the wheels are rolling,
On to Montana,
Through Kansas and Iowa.

WEAVERS AND MEN: Hey, prairie man,
Hey, prairie man,
He's gonna (hey!) take 'em on the Santa Fe,
Overland, Oregon trail, he will
And the people will sing a ballad about him,
And call him "Buffalo Bill,"
"Jim Bridger," "Kit Carson" . . .
Hey!
Let the weavers of legend make him tall,
Let the weavers of legend make him strong,
Let the weavers of legend make him real.
Let all the weavers make him real,
All the weavers . . .

ACT ONE

WEAVERS *have pulled a man from their midst, and are busy putting the finishing touches on him.*

WEAVER MAN #1: *(Presenting the new hero, a tall, leaderly type of* WAGON MAN.*)* And we'll call him . . . Donner.

DONNER: *(Trying out the name)* Donner.

WEAVER #1: George Donner, it has a ring of destiny.

GEORGE DONNER *considers this, nods, then goes to organize the men.*

WEAVER #1: He's a good man, and well-meaning. And how tall he is—his shadow reaches across the prairies and into California!

THE MEN *have been conversing among themselves, and now* GEORGE DONNER *steps from the group and addresses the* WEAVERS.

DONNER: I'm afraid there's a problem. The men want women, now.

MEN: *(Raising a commotion)* That's telling 'em, Donner! We want women!

DONNER *turns and holds out his hand to* BARBARA ALLEN, *who immediately shrinks back and clings to* HOPPIN' JOHN.

HOPPIN' JOHN: We're settling here, awhile. Besides, she's not fit for the kind of life out there.

MEN: *(Protesting)* Then, who'll cook for us! And sew for us! And read to us at night?!

A man needs a woman
To bear his sons,
And sons of sons.
A woman to travel
By his side
And be his new country bride . . .

They refuse to move any further.

HOPPIN' JOHN: Fine. But you'll need a woman made of stronger stuff than this one.

The grey dawn has given way to the pinks and oranges of sunrise. And now, silhouetted against the sky there appears the figure of ANNE

HUTCHINSON. *But she is changed, and now suggests a cloaked and bonneted woman of the mid-19th century.*

DONNER: *(Softly, in awe)* Could the weavers of legend
Make her real . . . ?

THE WEAVERS *are already doing just that, and sing.*

WEAVERS: Woman of stone,
Woman of stone,
There's a new life before you,
And you must be strong.
Sweet was your love,
Let it be known;
But cast it away,
For now you're of stone.
Cast it away,
Or cast it in stone.

THE WOMAN: *(Coming to life)* You sail in on a sea worn ship
To a wild, new land,
And it sits and broods and watches
As you anchor in the rushes.
Through the winter you live
With the fear
Of the empty and black and God only knows,
But you know there's no returning,
And you're here to stay, forever.

MEN: So you build a home,
And you make a fire,
And you put the kettle on:
Making gingerbread as you spin the thread
Of a new life at your wheel,
No more only a woman now,
Cut from the granite cliffs of these new hills,
Cut from the granite cliffs of these new hills,
You're cut from the granite cliffs of these new hills.

THE WOMAN *has been removing her bonnet and cloak, and begins to move down towards the frontier.*

THE WOMAN: I'll fold away
On the back shelves of yesterday

ACT ONE

All things of summer-sweet pleasure;
Trading blue calico
For homespun and grey,
And velvet for brown shoe leather,
And velvet for brown shoe leather.

She is now dressed as a PIONEER WOMAN, *in earth colors, homespun and leather. Her face is set in the strong, serene expression that has been mirrored in so many photographs of the early Pioneer Women, arms folded, standing before their sod huts on The Plains.*

As she descends, HOPPIN' JOHN *catches her hand. Their eyes meet, and then he leads her to* DONNER.

HOPPIN' JOHN: George Donner, a wife for you.

WEAVER MAN #2: And her name will be . . . Tamson. Tamson Donner. *(Laughing)* Stiched up ten thousand dollar bills into a quilt, and set out with her husband and children in the biggest wagon going West!

WEAVER MAN #2 *hands* MRS. DONNER *the quilt just described. She accept the quilt, and she and* GEORGE *are now joined by* TWO CHILDREN.

DONNER: *(It is almost a proposal)* You move west in a wagon now,
To a wild, new land,
With the setting sun before you,
As you cross the haunted prairie.
Overland, to Dakota you go,
Through the dust and the grass
Of a somewhere that nobody knows,
But you know there's no returning,
And you're moving on, together.

TAMSON DONNER *(She has heard the stories, nods)*
Then you stop, only once,
In the bone dry shade of a greasewood tree;
And on the prairie land,
You give silent birth
To a dark and hungry child.
But, you're more than a mother now,
You're hewn from the marble quarries of this land . . .

MEN: Hewn from the marble quarries of this land,
Hewn from the marble quarries of this land.

THE DONNER PARTY *has taken form, and now begins its slowly,
heroic journey West.*

DONNER, with MEN: Woman of stone,
Woman of stone,
There's a new world before you,
And you must move on.
Sweet was our love,
Let it be known;
But cast it away,
For now you're of stone.
Cast it away,
Or cast it in stone.

Without a backward glance, MR. AND MRS. GEORGE DONNER *have gone out into the unknown. Other* PIONEER MEN *have been joined by other* WIVES, *and have joined the* DONNERS *in the Great Immigration.*

HOPPIN' JOHN *and* BARBARA *are now alone. There is silence and a sense of stillness, and* BARBARA *now begins to sing softly, making it a haunting entreaty.*

BARBARA: Let me fill your world with pretty things,
Let me fill your cup from sweet water springs;
We'll share and settle,
And plough the meadow,
And build a house
Where our first and last are born . . .

Staging indicates that they have now surrounded themselves with four walls, one of which features a large, opened window.

HOPPIN' JOHN: A house on the edge of the Prairie . . .
(He sings) With a window on the West,
Where I can watch the people passing by,
Like a river rolling west,
Reaching out from far beyond the eastern sky . . .

(He stares out the window, imagining the passing parade)
All the people, God bless the people,
They keep on coming,

They keep on moving across the land.
And it's all in their hands, my love,
And it's all in their hands.

BARBARA: *Gently, trying to coax his attention towards their own, domestic situation now)*
Stop counting miles awhile,
And maybe we can stand
And count the stars awhile . . .

HOPPIN' JOHN: *(Paying no attention to her, but drawn to his window where he continues painting the pictures he sees in his mind's eyes.)*
Comes Brigham Young
With his wagons strung
To the Deseret sands in the Salt Lake Valley;
The Rockies, the Wasatch,
The Wind River Mountains are calling!
Hey,
The Wind River Mountains are calling!

Bring Concord coaches,
And Conestogas,
Pushcarts, handcarts,
Bring anything that rolls!
Bring anything that rolls!

Come "Hoosier" gals
And "Green Mountain Boys,"
"Buckeyes" and "Pikes,"
It's time to get moving,
The first day of summer
Is blooming all over the land,
Is blooming all over the land!

BARBARA: *(Increasingly concerned)*
I'll sew you a shirt of linsey-woolsey,
Quilt you a blanket warm and downy,
And weave pretty baskets—

HOPPIN' JOHN: *(Calling out to imagined passing wagons)* Where are you going?

Around the stage, PLAYERS *answer, assuming various characterizations.*

WAGON MASTER: California!

WAGON MASTER'S WIFE: Going to see the elephant!

HOPPIN' JOHN: *(To another group)* Where you going?

WAGON MASTER #2: Utah Territory!

HOPPIN' JOHN: Where you going?

WAGON MASTER #3: Arizona Territory!

HOPPIN' JOHN *is obviously yearning after the passing wagons, desperate to be joining.* BARBARA *comes up behind him, not insisting, trying to be understanding about it.*

BARBARA: *(Softly)* I thought that we might bide awhile,
And set the dreams aside, awhile.

HOPPIN' JOHN: *(Tentatively)* Yes. Of course . . . *(He catches her hand, lovingly, and tries to make her share his enthusiasm for it all.)*
But the people, God bless the people,
They keep on coming,
They keep on settling across the land.
And it's all in their hands, my love,
And it's all in their hands, my love,
And it's all in their hands . . .

Outside, SETTLERS *have begun to arrive, gathering in a tableau around the stage. One by one they have been adding a chorale harmony to the final stanzas of* HOPPIN' JOHN's *song.*

Now, SETTLERS *begin to break the tableau as underscoring continues. A* SETTLER MAN *ambles past the window and calls out a friendly greeting to* HOPPIN' JOHN.

SETTLER MAN: Mornin', neighbor!

HOPPIN' JOHN: Mornin'. *(He calls to* BARBARA*)* Hey, there's folks begun to settle here. We're gonna be a town, soon!

BARBARA *comes to the window. Two* SETTLER WOMEN *are strolling by, and nod cheerfully to* BARBARA.

SETTLER WOMAN: Good afternoon, neighbor.

BARBARA: Good afternoon . . . *(She smiles, savouring the word)* Neighbors!

ACT ONE

HOPPIN' JOHN *goes out the door to converse with the* SETTLER MAN. *Meanwhile,* WEAVER MAN #1 *has taken on the characterization of a very old* PEDDLER MAN, *and comes wandering past the window. He calls up to* BARBARA.

PEDDLER MAN: Fresh corn, Ma'am? The first of summer. And ripe watermelons, and blackberries... *(Several* SETTLER WOMEN *gather and select from the imaginary produce.* PEDDLER MAN *continues to extoll the virtues of his wares.)* Fresh pumpkins and squash, the first of Autumn. And the ripest, crispest, juiciest apples this side of the Ohio!

CHILDREN *have begun to gather, and now* HOPPIN' JOHN *ambles over towards the* PEDDLER.

HOPPIN' JOHN: *(Producing a coin)* The apples sound good.

PEDDLER MAN: Are good. Planted 'em myself, just across the river, nigh onto twenty years ago.

As HOPPIN' JOHN *loads up on the apples, the* CHILDREN *gather around him, and he begins to pass the apples among them. The* PEDDLER MAN, *without having accepted the coin, smiles and moves away, dropping his characterization and returning to his position among the* WEAVERS. HOPPIN' JOHN *looks after him, musing, then speaks to the children.*

HOPPIN' JOHN: I s'pose you all know who that old man was, now?

CHILDREN: 'Twere the peddler man, sir. And thank 'ee for the apples!

HOPPIN' JOHN: *(With a laugh)* Don't thank me. Thank that old "peddler man," who was no peddler at all. That was Johnny Appleseed!

CHILDREN: For a fact!

They begin to scamper after the peddler, calling out to him, but HOPPIN' JOHN *stops them with a laugh.*

HOPPIN' JOHN: Whoah! He's long gone from this earth. That was only his legend, walked by.

BARBARA *has returned to the house, and now appears at the window, smiling at the warm picture of her* HUSBAND *and the* CHILDREN.

CHILDREN: *(In awe, to one another)* 'Twere Johnny Appleseed.

HOPPIN' JOHN: Some take from the land, but he gave. He gave the gift of life.

CHILDREN: *(Chiming in brightly, singing what might be for them a traditional song.)* From a cider press in Pennsylvania,
To the hills of Indiana,
Hey, Johnny, ho, Johnny Appleseed's a-comin'
Hey, Johnny, sing, John, Johnny, sing, hey!

The stage has been flooded with leaf projections, giving the impression that the flatlands are blooming with new life.

CHILDREN: Spring, blossom,
Summer, green;
Autumn, red, and
Winter, russet:
How bright the changing
Fruit of the apple tree,
That brings the changing
Seasons to me!

THE CHILDREN, *biting into their apples, now run out in the direction recently taken by* THE PEDDLER, *waving their goodbyes to* HOPPIN' JOHN. BARBARA *starts to come outside now, then sees* HOPPIN' JOHN *move into a realm of his own, his manner darkening. She hesitates, then steps back.*

HOPPIN' JOHN: *(Musing)* How bright the changing
Fruit of the apple tree,
That brings the changing
Seasons to me . . .
But seasons change, and saplings grow,
In the orchards, planted row upon row;
And then come men with pretty young wives,
Split log cabins and family lives,
And then comes time for Johnny to move,
For Johnny to go a-drifting.
He's a loner, and nothing will change him,
Nothing will ever change him . . .

He is singing about himself now, and BARBARA *knows this. Troubled, she quietly goes back inside, leaving him alone.* SEVERAL SETTLER

ACT ONE

WOMEN *have now gathered beneath* BARBARA's *window, and they sing in sympathy with regard to the brooding* HOPPIN' JOHN.

WOMEN: Johnny lookin' for the sun,
Lookin' for the moon,
Lookin' for the rainbow roads to heaven,
Scatters the strings of everyday things,
And moves on . . .
Johnny, Johnny, Hoppin' John.

Johnny gathers up the wind,
Gathers up the rain,
Gathers all the bright, white stars of summer.
Then he plants the seeds of apples and dreams,
And he's gone;
Johnny, Johnny, Hoppin' John.

But Johnny never sees his apple trees grow,
And Johnny never smells the blossoms in bloom;
And Johnny never tastes the sweet, ripe pippins
That fall in September . . .

HOPPIN' JOHN: And shall I never drink the cider from my tree?
And will I never know my daughters and my sons?
And must I plant the seed, and watch the roots begin,
Then turn away from them forever?

(He gets up) Well, set out my boots for walking,
And call me Hoppin' John.
And if I never come this way again,
I'll never know what may have been.

Johnny, lookin' for the sun,
Lookin' for the moon,
Lookin' for the rainbow roads to heaven;
Scatter the strings of everyday things, and you're gone.
Johnny, Johnny, Hoppin' John.
Johnny, Johnny, Hoppin' John.

As if from a peg outside the door, he gathers a coat and cap. Through the large window, he catches sight of BARBARA, *head bent, perhaps hiding tears. Sadly, he blows her a silent kiss, then turns to go off.* BARBARA *looks up, her hand touching her cheek, as if she has felt his last kiss. She is dry eyed, although it's clear that she fully understands he has left her. She sings because she doesn't fully understand his reasons.*

BARBARA: Grasshopper,
There you go wandering,
Over brown meadows and valleys of stone.
Grasshopper,
When will you
When will you rest in a nest of your own,
Rest in a nest of your own?

Grasshopper,
Spring turns to summer,
Then summer to winter, when fires burn low.
Grasshopper,
Winter is coming now.
Where will you go when the rain turns to snow,
Where, when the rain turns to snow?

(She gets up and wanders through the open door, letting her eyes take in the melancholy sweep of the landscape.)
Grasses are greener, beyond the far fences,
Across the grey prairies to distant, black hills.
So, you go wandering to reach the far fences,,
And find . . . you've left something behind.

The other WOMEN *have slowly, silently come up, and now gather around to join her in scanning the wide prairie. For a moment, they seem to be the same women who scanned the seas off Cape Cod a hundred years earlier.*

BARBARA AND WOMEN: Grasshopper,
What are you looking for?
If you should find it, then how will you know?
Something forgotten, or something remembered,
A part of a dream that was lost, long ago,
Lost, where the prairie winds blow . . .

In the distance, HOPPIN' JOHN *is silhouetted against what has become an early October sky. A chill wind sweeps across the prairie, bringing with it the first taste of winter.* HOPPIN' JOHN *gathers his coat close about him as* BARBARA *and the* WOMEN *come to rest in a melancholy, yearning tableau.*

Act One

During these last scenes, The Weavers *have slowly been working their collective way out of the tapestry and back to their loom. As the lights begin to fade on the people in the tapestry, we are aware of a soft shuffling and murmuring from among the* Weavers.

Weaver Woman: And there. We've used up almost a whole basket of thread.

Weaver Man #1: It'll take a short while to spin some new.

Weaver Man #2: We've done plenty enough for the first sitting, anyhow.

He looks down at the tapestry, supposedly seeing the tableau, highlighting Hoppin' John *now, his face turned west and catching the glow of the setting sun. The other* Weavers *also study the tapestry.*

Weaver Man #1: How did he get caught up in it!

Weaver Man #2: I suppose there's no stopping him, now.

Weaver Woman: And what lies ahead, I don't like to think of.

The others nod, reflecting upon this. Softly, singing a last, echoing coda, Barbara *and the* Women *sing.*

Barbara and Women: Hoppin' John
Hoppin' John
Hoppin' John . . .

Hoppin' John *begins to move West as the lights slowly fade to darkness.*

END OF ACT ONE

Act Two

At Rise: WEAVER WOMAN *is seated at the loom, and the two* WEAVER MEN *now amble in to rejoin her.*

WEAVER WOMAN: While you were away, I wove the trail west.

WEAVER MAN #1: *(surveying the tapestry)* More dark colors, I see.

WEAVER WOMAN: *(Controlling her irritation)* The brown represents broken wagon wheels; and the touches of black are for all the unmarked graves along the way.

WEAVER MAN #2: *(Unloading an imaginary basket)* We've brought several new colors.

WEAVER MAN #1: *(Sitting to weave)* Where are we, now?

WEAVER WOMAN: That's the Donner party, and these are the High Sierras. We can use your green for pine forests . . . and white, lots of white, for gently falling snow.

Lights have revealed the PLAYERS *in a tableau representing the* DONNER PARTY's *High Sierra camp. Several of the group's members are in frozen, stylized positions that suggest gravestones. Prominent among these is* GEORGE DONNER.

MRS. DONNER *has the* TWO CHILDREN *before her, and she is slowly repeating a phrase to them, which the* CHILDREN *and* PLAYERS *echo like a round.*

MRS. DONNER: We are the children of
Mr. and Mrs. George Donner . . .

CHILDREN: We are the children of
Mr. and Mrs. George Donner . . .

PLAYERS: We are the children of
Mr. and Mrs. George Donner . . .

MRS. DONNER: *(To her children)* Your father is gone now, do you understand? And if something should happen to me, it's

Act Two

very important that you remember. *(She smiles, trying to make a game of it)* We are the children of
Mr. and Mrs. George Donner . . .

(She is wrapping each child in imaginary layers of extra clothing.) Mrs. Reed will take you to the rescue camp, but you must hurry before the next snowfall. I'll stay with your father until help comes.

Mrs. Reed, *a member of the group, gathers up the children.* Mrs. Donner *kisses each one goodbye, knowing it is the last she will see of them, then watches as they weave their way through the falling dusk. As this is happening, various voices from the dead call to her, softly.*

George Donner: Tamson, come to sleep, now.

Mrs. Donner: *(Wearily)* Come to die, you mean.

George Donner: Journey's end, Tamson. And it's so peaceful here.

Other Players: Mrs. Donner . . . ! Tamson Donner . . . !

Mrs. Donner: *(Smiles ruefully, then sings)*
The snow in the mountains will sweep down and cover us,
Sweep down and bury us, cold and alone.
And can this be the ending for we who went wandering
To find . . . there was nothing to find?

She takes the quilt and wraps it around herself, then drifts into sleep. But the Weavers *will have none of this. They get up from their loom, and work their way through the frozen graveyard, singing with increasing vigor.*

Weavers: Ships sail in, and they sail sway.
Cities rise, and they turn to clay.
But people keep the bright fires burning,
And people keep the millwheels turning,
And through it all, I see through it all,
The silver threads of learning.

They have reached Mrs. Donner *and are coaxing her to life again. She slowly responds.*

Weavers: Young Mrs. Donner was buried today,

But women of stone live on, they say.
The seeds of summer that fall in autumn,
Sweepin' through the winter, will bloom another spring,
And we'll call her "Annie Christmas,"
Or call her "Barbara Frietchie,"
Or call her "Brave Eliza,"
Wake up, stand up tall!

MRS. DONNER *is now bolt upright.*

WEAVERS: What really matters is the spirit
That we're weaving through them all.

MRS. DONNER: *(with new vigor)* Walking tall, walking tall, my spirit!

WEAVERS: *(Encouraging her)* Walking tall, walking tall, my soul!

MRS. DONNER: All my daughters and sons,
Come open your eyes and see,
In the generations passing,
There is something everlasting walking on:
Something inside that never will die lives,
And you're walking tall, my spirit,
Walk around this old world, walk tall!
Forever, yes my spirit,
Forever, yes my soul!

As she sings, one by one the dead are beginning to respond, awakening and joining into her song.

AWAKENED DEAD: Walking tall, walking tall, my spirit!
Walking tall, walking tall, my soul!

MRS. DONNER: Through all the siftings of sand,
And shiftings of moons and tides,
And through all the rearranging,
There is something never-changing shining on:
Something inside, through pleasures and pains remains,
And you're shining bright, my spirit,
Shine around this old world, shine bright.
Forever, yes my spirit,
Forever, yes my soul!

ACT TWO

In the distance, HOPPIN' JOHN *has appeared, and now he begins to work his way down to* MRS. DONNER, *calling to her.*

HOPPIN' JOHN: Mrs. Donner . . . Tamson Donner!

MRS. DONNER: *(Without emotion, points to the area where the camp had been)* Mrs. Donner is dead now. How she endured this much, I'll never know. *(She take his hand)* But I'm glad you've come this far—there's so much to be done, now! *(She surveys the scene, taking in the view of the dead who are yet to awaken.)*
And, though my grave is cold and shallow,
And rude is my cross,
Cut from the branch of a juniper,
I shall have no sorrow . . .

For the bells, how hollow they toll,
The death of an empty shell;
It's not a time for grieving,
But an hour of renewing!
Oh, something inside that never will die lives,
And you're walking tall, my spirit,
Walk around this old world, walk tall!
Forever, yes my spirit.

She is joined by the remainder of the AWAKENED DEAD.

MRS. DONNER AND AWAKENED DEAD: Forever . . .
And ever . . .
And ever . . .
Yes, my soul!

As the dead have awakened, MRS. DONNER *has sent them off with great exhilaration, as though to do great things in the west.*

Her triumph, however, is now clouded by an agitated buzzing sound, which now grows louder, insistent and irritating. She covers her ears and looks to HOPPIN' JOHN *for an explanation.*

MRS. DONNER: What in God's name is that awful racket!

HOPPIN' JOHN: Locust!

MRS. DONNER: What . . . ?

HOPPIN' JOHN: *(Shouting to be heard)* Like locusts, they're coming. I passed 'em on the prairie, all of 'em, come racing across the land with no thought at all of where they're going, or what they're doing . . .

MRS. DONNER: But who *are* they?

HOPPIN' JOHN: Locusts, I said—raping the land!

MRS. DONNER: *(With a scornful laugh and a glance at the bleak, rather unpromising land.) Of what?*

Her question is answered as a scraggily, almost cartoon-like bunch of FORTY-NINERS *comes bustling across, singing and whining in shrill voices as they clatter their way to California.*

FORTY-NINERS: There are
Pockets of gold and silver,
Pockets of gold and silver,
Pockets of gold and silver there!

Pickin' up a pick and pan,
Packin' up a jenny mule;
Headin' for the open prairie,
Carvin' our initials, Mary-
Jo, on Independence Rock,
With plenty o' luck
That's where I'm goin', goin', goin'!
(Goin', goin' gone)
To them
Pockets of gold and silver,
Pockets of gold and silver,
Pockets of gold and silver, there!

Headin' for the High Sierra,
Down the American River;
Stoppin' off in Sacramento,
Pickin' up a bright memento,
Takin' it to San Francisco,
Meltin' it down to precious coin, coin, coin!
(Goin', Goin', Gone!)
To them
Pockets of gold and silver
Pockets of gold and silver,
Pockets of gold and silver in them hills . . . !

ACT TWO

Like obnoxious pests, they have swept across the land, but the agitation they have created remains, and both HOPPIN' JOHN *and* MRS. DONNER *are not untouched by it.*

MRS. DONNER: Well, if this is the new trend, we'd best adapt to it. I'm not going to be left behind if everyone else is suddenly becoming wealthy off the land!

HOPPIN' JOHN: *(With an appreciative laugh)* And no need to go all the way to California for it—there's plenty, all around us!

MRS. DONNER: There certainly is! *(She has snatched up the quilt, and begins to rip it apart)* She sewed up ten thousand dollars in here!

HOPPIN' JOHN: *(Another laugh, sings expansively)*
I'll build a city in Nevada, for you, my love,
Where all the silver in the foothills shines through, my love;
Between the green Sierra Pines,
The Truckee River is a-falling free,
And pebbles are washed, and rushed to the sea,
Leaving silver and gold for you . . . and me.

Several PLAYERS *have begun to transform themselves into* MINERS *and* PROSPECTORS, *and the gathering group begins to sing, staging themselves to suggest a stylized mining town.*

MINERS: In Virginia City,
The silver runs deep, and the gals ain't pretty.
In Virginia City,
The Colt 45 sings a mighty mean ditty.
In Virginia City,
The red-eye's a dollar a shot, and shitty,
But I'm gonna make Virginia City my home.

In Virginia City,
It's a five card stud so-cie-itty;
In Virginia City,
There's a rule of poker pro-prie-itty:
In Virginia City,
The winner is hung by a town committee,
But I'm gonna make Virginia City my home.

Now, I don't mind,
Bunkin' with a bevy of fleas,

Walkin' the streets,
And sinkin' in mud to my knees.
Don't mind if the coffee
And the hominy's gritty,
In Virginia City,
'Cause I'm down in the mines, all morning,
And down at the mint, all day.
A bowl of cream will feed the kitty,
But silver feeds Virginia City!

And,
In Virginia City,
They cuss, and they curse, and the jokes ain't witty;
In Virginia City,
There ain't much shame, and there ain't much pity.
In Virginia City,
There ain't no ass, and there ain't no titty!
But I'm gonna make Virginia City my home.
In Virginia City, I'm a-settlin'
In Virginia City, I'm a-settlin'
In Virginia City, I'm a-settlin' ma'am, hot damn!
In Virginia City,
In Virginia City,
In Virginia City, yes I am!

HOPPIN' JOHN *and* MRS. DONNER *have moved in, and are sizing up the situation.*

MRS. DONNER: I've got a feeling . . .

MINERS: Yes, Ma'am?

MRS. DONNER: Something is needed here . . .

MINERS: Yes, Ma'am!

MRS. DONNER: Such a sad and lonely town,
With only lonely men needs me!

MINERS: *(Enthusiastically)* Yes, Ma'am!

MRS DONNER: Well, come on, you weavers of legend
Make me bold and fancy-dancin' now;
Dress me fine, and call me Madame!

ACT TWO

MINERS: Madame! (MRS. DONNER *is changing now, and quickly becomes* JULIA BULETTE, *an elegant Madame of the Old West*)

JULIA BULETTE: And I'll be Queen of the Comstock,
Brave, legendary Julia Bulette
Will set the West on sweet, sweet fire!

JULIA and MEN: Fire, sweet, sweet fire!

WEAVER MEN; When Julia Bulette came into town,
Everybody settled down!

WEAVER WOMAN: *(The male weavers are getting out of hand)* Settle down!

Young, pretty PROSTITUTES *are beginning to arrive.*

MINERS: She brought a bevy of cathouse ladies,
And dressed 'em all in silk and satin,
And built a row of clap-board cottages,
And lit 'em all with bright, red lanterns!

PROSTITUTES: *(Strutting by)*
Saturday night, 'round a quarter past ten,
That's where you'll find Virginia City men,
Everybody's going down round sportin' row!

JULIA: Y'all come on down to Julia's Palace, now!

MINERS: *(Following the girls)*
Julia Bulette, light yer bright, red light,
Virginia City ladies are walkin' tonight,
And everybody's goin' down,
Goin' down 'round sportin' row!

DIGNIFIED MATRONS *have now appeared on the scene. They stand to one side, and are shocked and disapproving.*

MATRONS: *(Pointing to the goings-on in horror)*
Can that extravaganza be
What all the fussing's for?
That so-called big bonanza
Behind that bolted door
Is just the village whore!!

MATRON #1: I swear, the men have all gone crazy. Yesterday, they made her an honorary member of the Fire Department!

MATRON #2: Yes, well, tomorrow they're naming a railroad car after her.

MATRON #1: Hm. The sleeping car, no doubt.

MINERS: Listen, listen, listen,
Now, can't you hear it?
Listen, listen, listen,
Now, can't you hear it?

(They whisper in tempo, so that it sounds like the clickity-clack of railroad wheels)

Julia Bulette!
Julia Bulette!
Julia Bulette!
There goes the
Virginia and Truckee Railroad,
Virginia and Truckee Railroad,
Rollin' out the legend of the Comstock,
Beatin' out the ballad of the Comstock!
Listen to the rattlin' rollin'
Virginia and Truckee Railroad,
Callin' her the belle o' the Comstock,
Makin' her the queen o' the Comstock,
Callin' her the belle o' the Comstock,
Makin' her the queen o' the Comstock lode!

JULIA *begins to lead everyone in a wild dance.*

JULIA: Come on, you high-hoofin' men,
Step it light, light, light,
Hold 'em tight, tight, tight,
The fiddler is a-tunin' up
And I got a feelin' we'll be Virginia Reelin'
In Virginia City, tonight!

In the din of the music, we hear faint scratches of the Devil's violin.

PROSTITUTES and MINERS: Come on, you high-hoofin' men,
Step it light, light, light,
Hold 'em tight, tight, tight,
The fiddler is a-tunin' up,
And I got a feelin' we'll be Virginia Reelin'
In Virginia City tonight!

ACT TWO

ENSEMBLE: Now,
In Virginia City,
The silver's all mine, and the gals are pretty!
And in Virginia City,
The ragtime piano plays a mighty fine ditty!
And, in Virginia City,
Plenty o' ass and plenty o' titty,
And I'm gonna make Virginia City my home!
In Virginia City, I'm a-settlin'
In Virginia City, I'm a-settlin'
In Virginia City, I'm a-settlin' ma'am, hot damn!
In Virginia City,
In Virginia City,
In Virginia City, yes I am!

By the end of the number, Virginia City is a shambles. The peak of color and gaiety it had achieved midway in the song is no more; PROSTITUTES *are lolling in the streets,* DRUNKS *are face-down in the mud, and definite strains of darkness and despair have begun to weave themselves into the picture again.*

HOPPIN' JOHN *looks around at what he has created, and grows disgusted and discouraged. And, as if called up in his memory, in vivid contrast to the ugliness around him, the image of* BARBARA ALLEN *appears.*

BARBARA: *(Softly)* Let me fill your world with pretty things,
Let me fill your cup from sweet water springs . . .

HOPPIN' JOHN: *(Looking around, confused, disoriented, he sings)*
I built a city on the river,
And there, my love,
In the city of Saint Louie,
I left my love . . .
Beside the wind Missouri's shore,
Between the Mississippi and the sea;
Now, she walks and weaves,
And I wander lonely . . .

(JULIA BULETTE *has been sympathetic, but she is not about to dwell upon* HOPPIN' JOHN's *past love. With a friendly squeeze of his hand, she has moved off, leaving him alone with his thoughts.)*

In the city of Saint Louie,
She sleeps tonight, without me.
Does she think about me . . .

The image of BARBARA ALLEN *had faded away, but now she reappears, although very much changed: pale, wistful, less earthly than ever, she is dressed in flowing gown with her hair hanging loose. With tear-stained eyes, she seems to be searching the empty night.*

HOPPIN' JOHN: *(In dismay, to the* WEAVERS*)* But she's so . . . changed! Who has she become?

WEAVER WOMAN: *(A hint of reproach in her voice)* A legend about lost love.

WEAVERS: *(Sing)* On the Louisiana Bayou,
There's an Acadian tale they tell;
There's where the fair "Evangeline"
Does dwell,
Separated in the Seven Year's War
From her sweet love, Gabriel.

All memory of Virginia City and the West has faded away, and now EVANGELINE's *world begins to flood the stage in colors of lichens and Spanish moss.*

WEAVERS: He was taken away from her
On a long-gone day,
Taken somewhere, nobody knows.
But still, she goes searching,
Up river, down, ever asking as she goes . . .

EVANGELINE: *(As she begins her quest, stopping to ask some* CAJUN GIRLS*)* Keelboat, paddlewheel, on the river,
Do you know where my love has gone?

CAJUN GIRLS: He passed here yesterday,
Left here, yesterday,
Said he was moving on . . .

EVANGELINE *now wanders on her legendary journey as the* CAJUN GIRLS *sing her ballad.*

CAJUN GIRLS: He's gone where the rivers take him,
Down, through the mountains to the sea.

ACT TWO

Go, Evangeline,
Fly, Evangeline,
And, Evangeline,
You'll find him there,
Where the rivers take him,
On through the valley of the hill.
Sail, Evangeline,
On, Evangeline,
And, Evangeline,
You'll find him still.

Where Evangeline goes, you can see her;
That's Evangeline, by the river,
With a lantern of fireflies, she goes,
Through the sycamore and the linden,
Through the Wachita willows,
Where the cedar and the cypress
Echo whispers in the wind:

MEN'S VOICES: "Evangeline," they call. "Evangeline"!

CAJUN GIRLS: Go on, where the rivers take you,
Down through the Bayou to the bay.
Drift, Evangeline,
Glide, Evangeline,
Row, Evangeline . . .
His love is true, and he waits for you.

RIVER MEN *gather, as if on the riverbank, catching* EVANGELINE *as she drifts by.*

RIVER MEN: White were the waters of the Nebraska,
Blue were the waters of the Ohio;
Brown were the waters of the Missouri,
But Black are the waters of the Mississippi . . .

CAJUN GIRLS: She stops in all the river cities,
Even searching cemeteries,
Fearful that she'll find his name
Engraved on a lonely stone . . .

EVANGELINE: Have you seen him?

CAJUN GIRLS: Yes, Evangeline!

EVANGELINE: Did he stop here?

CAJUN GIRLS: Yes, Evangeline!

EVANGELINE: Did he stay here?

CAJUN GIRLS: No, Evangeline, No . . .
He's gone where the rivers take him,
West, through the prairies to the sea;
Run, Evangeline,
Fly, Evangeline,
And, Evangeline, you'll find him there,
Where the rivers take him,
As they were ever meant to do.
Sail, Evangeline,
On, Evangeline,
For, Evangeline,
His love is true, and he waits for you.
Evangeline, sail on, Evangeline . . .
Somewhere, he waits for you,
Somewhere, he waits for you,
Somewhere, he waits . . .

EVANGELINE, *broken and confused, falls to her knees on the riverbank.*

HOPPIN' JOHN: *(Helpless from his distant vantage point, cries out to the* WEAVERS*)* But, what are you doing? Everything is wrong now—can't you stop it?

WEAVER WOMAN: *(Genuinely helpless, as the* WEAVERS' *fingers continue to fly over the loom)* We can't stop . . . we never could.

HOPPIN' JOHN: Then, let me out—I must get back to her.

WEAVER MAN #1: We can't. The tapestry is as it's woven, and you're a part of it.

HOPPIN' JOHN: *(Quietly)* I belong with her . . . we belong together.

WEAVER WOMAN: Recent events seem to have dictated otherwise . . .

Around EVANGELINE, *a quartet of* MINSTRELS *has begun to gather, swarming like deadly flies. As they enter, they pantomime putting on makeup, and their theatrical manner is readily apparent. They regard the forlorn* EVANGELINE *with jaundiced eyes.*

MINSTREL #1: "Evangeline?" When did we add *that* to the repertoire?

MINSTREL #2: It's by Longfellow.

MINSTREL #3: Very highbrow.

MINSTREL #4: Well, she's terrible in the role.

MINSTREL #1: She lacks style.

MINSTREL #2: She lacks talent.

MINSTREL #3: She lacks burnt cork, is what she lacks.

MINSTREL #4: *(Snapping at* EVANGELINE*)* Make up, dear! Costume! Don't dawdle between scenes!

MINSTREL #1: Your Little Eva number is next!

MINSTREL #2: It's not all glamour behind the footlights, you know.

They have moved in close to her, prodding and snatching at her. EVANGELINE *gets up, dazed and weary.*

EVANGELINE: Where has gentility gone?

MINSTREL #1: South, my dear.

MINSTREL #2: Way down upon the Swanee River.

MINSTREL #3: Gone South, along with romance and other lovely things.

MINSTREL #4: Such as yourself.

MINSTREL #1: You belong here.

MINSTREL #2: We claim you.

MINSTREL #3: As our very own!

They embrace her.

MINSTREL #4: Lovely!

MINSTREL #1: Precious!

MINSTREL #2: Enchanting!

MINSTREL #3: Divine!

EVANGELINE: *(Being pawed by one, then another, grows frightened)* Gentlemen, be seated!

MINSTREL #4: No, no, you belong to us now!

EVANGELINE: *(Hotly)* I belong to no one. I had the misfortune to love one man once, and I shall never love another!

MINSTREL #3: Your accent has become decidedly Southern, my dear.

MINSTREL #1: *(Calling the chaos to order)* Gentlemen! As the lady said, be seated.

He has been improvising an auction block, and suddenly EVANGELINE *realizes she is being treated as a piece of property. The proceedings have taken on the air of a tobacco auction, and that's precisely what they become, with* MINSTREL #1 *assuming the role of an* AUCTIONEER *now.*

AUCTIONEER: throw out your greenbacks,
And put down your bluebacks,
And let the biddin' begin for this good-lookin' gal.
She was lately a daughter of her Uncle Sam,
But now she's our own Cousin Sal!

MINSTRELS: Cousin Sal, Cousin Sal, Cousin Sal,
Confederate gal, our Cousin Sal!

They are getting out of hand in their appreciation of her charms.

AUCTIONEER: Gentlemen, we are civilized, so let's conduct ourselves accordingly!

Order is restored.

MINSTREL #2: Well, I'll bid one dollar, then.

AUCTIONEER: And it's a one dollar bid
From the man in the Panama hat
From Raleigh, North Carolina!

MINSTREL #3: Two!

ACT TWO 47

AUCTIONEER: Two dollar bid from the man
In the pongee suit
From Macon, Georgia!

MINSTREL #4: Three.

AUCTIONEER: And a three dollar bid
From the man in the calico shirt
From Charleston, South Carolina!

MINSTREL #2: Four!

AUCTIONEER: Four dollar bid
From the gentleman in from
Memphis, Tennessee!

MINSTRELS: It's a four dollar bid,
It's a four dollar bid,
It's a five dollar bid,

AUCTIONEER: Five dollar bid, five dollar bid, five dollar?

MINSTREL #3: Five dollars.

AUCTIONEER: Five dollar, five, I've
Heard five dolar
Come from Tallulah, Louisiana!

MINSTREL #4: Six . . . dollars!

AUCTIONEER: Six dollar
From a right fine feller
From Charlottesville, Virginia!

MINSTRELS: It's a six dollar bid,
It's a six dollar bid,
It's a seven dollar bid.

AUCTIONEER: Seven dollar bid, seven dollar bid, seven dollar?

MINSTREL #2: Seven dollars.

MINSTRELS: Seven dollar bid
From the man in the Panama hat
From Raleigh, North Carolina,
Eight dollar bid
From the man in the pongee suit

From Macon, Georgia,
It's an eight dollar bid,
It's an eight dollar bid,
It's a nine dollar bid!

AUCTIONEER: Nine dollars, gentlemen, nine dollars, do I hear nine? Nine, nine, nine, nine, nine, nine? *(He is getting no results, so goes into a sales pitch.)* Now, cotton's king,
And tobacco's queen,
And the sugarcane is sweet and green;
But they can't hold a candle, pal,
To our ol' Cousin Sal!!

MINSTRELS: *(Pinching, poking, examining her)*
Little lady, Louisiana lady,
Little lady, Louisiana lady!

MINSTREL #3: What the hell, nine dollars!

MINSTRELS: *(They are now being joined by gathering PLAYERS who are fascinated with the auction)*
Nine dollar bid
From the man in the calico shirt
From Charleston, South Carolina.
Ten dollar bid
From the gentleman in from
Memphis, Tennessee!

PLAYERS AND MINSTRELS: It's a twenty dollar bid,
It's a thirty dollar bid,
It's a forty dollar bid!

AUCTIONEER: Forty dollar bid, forty dollar bid, forty dollar?

MINSTREL #4: Forty dollars!

HOPPIN' JOHN *has been watching in horror, and has been attempting to bid throughout, but his voice has gone unheard.*

MINSTRELS AND PLAYERS: Forty dollar, forty,
I heard forty dollar
Come from Tallulah, Louisiana.
Fifty dollar from a right fine feller
From Charlottesville, Virginia!
It's a fifty dollar bid,

ACT TWO

Sixty dollar bid,
Seventy dollar bid!
It's an eighty dollar bid,
Ninety dollar bid,
One hundred dollars and she's
Sold!!!

AUCTIONEER: Sold to the gentlemen,
Everyone a gentleman,
Sold to the gentlemen of the South,
Sold, little lady,
Louisiana lady
To the legend of the South!

MINSTRELS: Sold to the chivalry, hospitality,
Sweet gentility of the South;
Sold, little lady,
Louisiana lady,
To the legend . . .

AUCTIONEER: You've been sold down the river
To the gentlemen of the South,
Little lady,
And they shall deliver you
To the legend of the South!

MINSTRELS: Little lady, Louisiana lady,
Little lady, Louisiana lady,
Sold down the river
To the gentlemen of the South,
Little lady,
And we shall deliver you
To the legend of the South!

MINSTRELS *take* EVANGELINE's *hand and promenade her to an area where* CREOLE GIRLS *flutter in with a giant, stylized hoop skirt, in which they proceed to dress her.*

CREOLES: She's
Becoming a belle of the delta,
Becoming a belle of the delta,
Becoming a delta belle, tonight.
Organdie up to here,

And crinoline out to there,
And whalebone laced up tight.
She's white as a magnolia,
Soft as a Creole tune,
And born to dance on the levee
By the light of a quarter moon . . .

EVANGELINE: *(Completely charmed with her new transformation)*
Camellias by the million,
Azaleas, all vermilion,
Are bloomin' at my cotillion ball.
Scattered around among those,
All the Jackson County beaux
Are at my beck and call . . .
Mint julep, if you please,
And a palmetto to fan my brow;
I'm
A daughter of Jefferson Davis,
A daughter of Jefferson Davis, now.

CREOLES: A daughter of Jefferson Davis,
Becoming a belle of the delta . . .

EVANGELINE: I'm
A daughter of Jefferson Davis,
A daughter of Jefferson Davis, now.

Staging suggests that EVANGELINE *is now at an elegant Southern ball, and all the* MINSTRELS *have become Southern gentlemen, bidding for her dance card as the bright polka of the Auction number reasserts itself.*

SOUTHERN GENTLEMEN: And it's a bid for the waltz, bid for the polka,
Bid for the last quadrille;
Bid for the Schottiche, bid for the Cakewalk,
And the Virginia Reel!
And she's
Sold to the gentlemen,
Everyone a gentleman,
Sold to the gentlemen of the South,
Sold, little lady, Louisiana lady
To the legend of the South!

ACT TWO

Sold to the chivalry, hospitality,
Sweet gentility of the South;
Sold, little lady, Louisiana lady
To the legend, you've been
Sold down the river to the gentlemen of the South,
Little lady,
And we shall deliver you
To the legend of the South!
Daughter of Jefferson Davis,
Daughter of Jefferson Davis,
Daughter of Jefferson Davis, now!

During the dance, HOPPIN' JOHN *has managed to work his way into the scene. Choreographically, he and* EVANGELINE *touch once, but the pattern of the dance separates them again, and he has been pulled out of the picture by the* WEAVERS.

EVANGELINE, *as if taking her hair down after the ball, is surrounded by several* CREOLE GIRLS, *and she sings wistfully.*

EVANGELINE: When all them sweet-talkin' men
Held me tight, tight, tight,
Steppin' light, light, light,
The fiddler played a dancin' tune,
But I've got a feelin' there'll be no Virginia reelin'
With my Virginia darlin' tonight.

She waltzes to a melancholy tune that is a variation of the WEAVERS' *theme, and we hear the sound of the* DEVIL's *violin.* THE CREOLE GIRLS *have come downstage and one speaks with foreboding. The lyrics are spoken, not in rhythm, but completely separate from the melancholy waltz that continues beneath the dialogue.*

CREOLE WOMAN: Late last night at the Quadroon Ball,
I heard a fiddler play.
He sat on top of a white pianna,
And he tuned up with "Oh, Susannah,"
And the room began to sway
Now, folks as far as Texarkana
Began to moan, and sing Hosannah,
And mosey on down Louisiana way;
And I thought, this music ain't no heav'nly manna,
But something dark, come outta the grey.

And I wiped my brow with my red bandanna,
And I knew, this devil shall have his due,
And we're about to pay.

(Music goes into tempo. She sings.) He's on the delta now,
Fiddling in the cotton,
Troubling up the moon.
Fresh from the cedar swamp
With his sweet violin.
He plays an old time melody,
But it sounds like "Dixie" to me;
He's gone to Natchez, now,
Pickin' up a drummer and a slide trombone man!

They hop a Cajun train,
Down to Alabama,
South to Mobile;
And all the brave young soldiers soon
Will dance to his song!
But he's got the beat to bend the blues,
So get up, get out, shout good news!

SOLDIER BOY: Ma, don't you understand?
I've got to join the band!
Got to play the trumpet
While the Devil plays Dixieland!

Staging of the number has a Showboat quality, but there is also something definitely military taking place. Now, several players suggest MUSICIANS *in a kind of jam session.*

MUSICIANS: When the Devil plays Dixieland,
All the catfish dance in the delta sand,
'Gators grin, begin to spin,
And get up to join the band.
He has a bullfrog bass quartet,
And an old jackrabbit on clarinet.
Hey, ain't it great, sugah, ain't it grand,
When the Devil plays Dixieland?

SOLDIERS: Beneath a Creole moon,
I finally found the rhythm,
Finally got the beat,
And all the fair young Georgia gals,

ACT TWO

My lord, how they sweeon!
But I don't need no Aura Lee,
I'd rather have a banjo on my knee!
To hell with what we planned,
I've gone to join the band!
Gone to play the bugle
When the devil plays Dixieland!

In the mounting chaos, HOPPIN' JOHN's *attempts to reach* EVANGELINE *have been further hampered. There is a choreographic division beginning to take place.*

MUSICIANS: When the Devil plays Dixieland,
He's got my old Kentucky mama in sweet demand.
Shoofly pies, catfish fries
Don't seem half so grand.
Get out your bright new cotton jeans,
There's a brand new rhythm from New Orleans;
Lift up your feet, sugah, take my hand,
When the devil plays Dixieland!

ENSEMBLE: *(A rousing finish)* He brought a ragtime rhythm from the River Styx,
Stride piano, and guitar picks;
Syncopation and red hot licks
Down to Dixieland!!

FOUR CREOLE GIRLS *gather downstage, alarmed at what they've done.*

GIRL #1: You conjured up the dancing devil!

GIRL #2: You conjured up the show!

GIRL #3: You conjured up his magic fiddle!

GIRL #4: You conjured up his bow!

ALL: We conjured up a heap o' trouble!
Call on Marie Laveau!
Call on Marie Laveau!

The WOMAN OF STONE *appears as voodoo queen,* MARIE LAVEAU.

MARIE LAVEAU: *(Demanding attention)* John Brown's body was cold in the grave,

PLAYERS: *(A quasi-revival meeting)*
Sing,
Hallelujah,
Sing!

MARIE LAVEAU: He hardly had time to grow old in the grave,

PLAYERS: Sing,
Hallelujah,
Sing!

MARIE LAVEAU: While he was sleepin'
In his bed,
You raised a ruckus
To wake the dead!
He sat up, and raised the lid;
And then that man did what Lazarus did!
John Brown's body is a-walkin' tonight!

PLAYERS: Sing,
Hallelujah,
Sing . . . !

Tempo changes, and JOHN BROWN'S BODY *is brought forth, as per the lyrics. He rises and begins to move among the people.*

PLAYERS: Hallelujah!
Hallelujah!
Hallelujah!
Hallelujah!

The proceedings have taken on a carnival atmosphere, and like a barker shouting out the various attractions, JOHN BROWN *begins an emotion-packed spiel, against which the* PLAYERS *continue tossing their "Hallelujah's".*

JOHN BROWN: There's a ship that's in from Africa,
With a cargo of despair,
And it sits in Charleston harbor,
And it fouls the water and fills the air
With the smell of fire and anger
While the foreman forges chains.
Her galley is full of dreams that died,
And the spirit of a people is caught inside;

ACT TWO

And in spite of the changing tide,
There she remains!

PLAYERS *have been getting more grotesque, perhaps donning masks at this point. Something mad and nightmarish is forming.*

PLAYERS: Get out your paint, and get out your powder,
Get out your bright dress, pretty lady.
Put on your beads and put on your bows
And come to the masquerade!
Put in your teeth, and after that, sir,
Put on your boots and high silk hat, sir.
Come as you can and come as you can't
And see how the game is played!

JOHN BROWN: A particular kind of madness
Begins to bloom and grow;
A peculiar institution;
And a book by Harriet Beecher Stowe
Don't paint a pretty picture,
And the people all say, no more!
And the North will cry for its abolition,
And the South will cling to its own tradition,
And they can't go on under this condition,
And so they cry for war!

PLAYERS: Get out your blue, and get out your grey,
And get out your bright new prety banner.
Get out your bugle, get out your drum
And come to the big parade!
Come as you are, or better,
Come as you were, or better,
Come as you might have been,
Come as you could have been,
Come as you meant to be!
Come as Ulysses S. Grant,
Or come as Robert E. Lee.
Come as Eliza, or come as Topsy,
Or come as Simon Legree!

JOHN BROWN: From Gettsyburg to Chickamauga
To Chickahominy Bridge,
To the bloody fields of Shiloh,

They lower the banner and muffle the drum,
And the orchards bloom in blossom
Where the men lay down to die.
And in the night, the deathwind blows,
Over the hills where the jasmine grows,
Over the graves in silent rows,
And who can tell me why?

PLAYERS: *(Choreographically, all has become a stylized battle, which rips and tears at the tapestry.)*
Get out your paint, and get out your powder,
Get out your bright dress, pretty lady.
Put on your beads and put on your bows
And come to the masquerade!
(Music grows discordant and out of tempo)
Put in your teeth, and after that, sir,
Put on your boots, and a high silk hat, sir . . .

They have created the spectre of Death. HOPPIN' JOHN *has broken through the discord, and it seems that he has been the one who finally rips the tapestry into separate parts, sending the* PLAYERS *sprawling.*

There is a moment of stillness.

EVANGELINE: *(Breaking the silence)* And all the red rockets
Were shot to the heavens,
And all the white stars
Came falling through . . .

WEAVERS: The legends we wove are all
Un-ravel-ling . . .

Their voices "unravel" and the tumbling, sprawling people have come to rest. All is still. HOPPIN' JOHN *looks around in dismay, then turns to the* WEAVERS, *broken and ashamed.*

HOPPIN' JOHN: You wove your mystic tapestry;
I watched your magic fingers fly.
Then I ripped it all to shreds,
And cast the broken threads
Against the waiting sky,
And watched the promise die . . .

WEAVERS *are unimpressed by this self-pitying confession, and have already set about to retrieve the scattered threads.*

ACT TWO

WEAVER WOMAN: *(Kindly)* Perhaps, to find what's locked within,
Some things must be opened wide . . .

WEAVER MEN: Don't turn away, my friend;
We'll patch, and weave, and mend.
The promise may have died,
But not the dream inside.

WEAVER WOMAN: You saw, of course, the pattern that was

HOPPIN' JOHN: Yes, and that's why I had to get out. The same things were happening to the same people, over and over again.

WEAVER WOMAN: Well, now that you see the pattern, wouldn't it be wonderful to work with the weave, instead of against it?

HOPPIN' JOHN: *(Somewhat surprised)* You're asking me to go on with you, after all I've done. But I'm not sure I want to.

WEAVER WOMAN: *(Indicating the baskets of yarn)* These are the colors of the future . . . see, they're not *all* dark.

EVANGELINE *and* THE WOMAN OF STONE *have been highlighted, and now they step forth, calling to* HOPPIN' JOHN *who seems to need further convincing.*

EVANGELINE AND WOMAN OF STONE: *(A gentle entreaty)*
Come, join us in the tapestry;
You'll find the way by looking back.
There's still so much undone,
The saga's just begun.

Come, weave and build and grow with us,
The brightest moments aren't all gone.
There's still some life, you see,
In this old tapestry;
Despite the break of dawn,
Some dreams linger on.

HOPPIN' JOHN: *(with growing understanding)*
Back where I come from,
I had to go

Back where it all began,
Back where the world was summertime new,
Robin's egg blue, every morning.
Where it is written
That yesterday
Only belongs to some?
I found a precious part of a dream
And hope for things to come,
Something forgotten was waiting,
Back where I'm from.

He moves in to join EVANGELINE *and* THE WOMAN. *One by one, the other* PLAYERS *in the tapestry begin to join into the song.*

HOPPIN' JOHN AND OTHERS: So many seasons of memory,
So many backroads to find,
Caught in the sunlight of my recollection.
So many faces recalling
Somebody I left behind;
Can it be I see my own reflection?
Where is it written
That yesterday
Only belongs to some?
I caught a precious glimpse of myself,
And of who I might become.
Something of value was waiting
Back where I'm from.

PLAYERS: *(Echoing)* Back where I come from,
Back where I come from,
Back where I come from.

WEAVERS *have moved back to their loom, and have begun weaving again. As they work and sing, the* PLAYERS *begin to move, recreating the tableau that began the show.*

WEAVERS: We'll patch a quilt on winter evenings,
Winter evenings, patterned and plain;

WEAVERS AND PLAYERS: And it seems to me, when the earth turns chill,

We'll be patching bright unmatching
Bit and pieces, still.
Weaving a tapestry, threaded with song
Stitched up and patched up
With legends that we were
So long gathering,
All a-gone gathering,
All summer long.

The lights slowly fade to darkness, as the WEAVERS *sing a gentle coda:*

Weaving a tapestry
Weaving a tapestry
Threaded with song
Threaded with song . . .

ALTERNATE LYRICS FOR "VIRGINIA CITY"

In Virginia City,
The silver runs deep, and the gals ain't pretty.
In Virginia City,
The Cold 45 sings a mighty mean ditty.
In Virginia City,
Rye's a dollar a shot, and the shot's itty-bitty,
But I'm gonna make Virginia City my home.

In Virginia City,
It's a five card stud so-cie-itty;
In Virginia City,
There's a rule of poker pro-prie-itty:
In Virginia City,
The winner is hung by a town committee,
But I'm gonna make Virginia City my home.

Now, I don't mind,
Bunkin' with a bevy of fleas,
Walkin' the streets,
And sinkin' in mud to my knees.
Don't mind if the coffee
And the hominy's gritty,
In Virginia City.
Cause I'm down in the mines, all morning,
And down at the mint, all day.
A bowl of cream will feed the kitty,
But silver feeds Virginia City!

And,
In Virginia City,
They fuss and they fume, and the jokes ain't witty;
In Virginia City,
There ain't much shame, and there ain't much pity.
In Virginia City,
Thre ain't no dames with names like "Kitty,"
But I'm gonna make Virginia City my home.

In Virginia City, I'm a settlin'
In Virginia City, I'm a settlin'
In Virginia City, I'm a settlin' ma'm, hot damn!
In Virginia City,
In Virginia City,
In Virginia City, yes I am!

MRS. DONNER: I've got a feeling . . .

MINERS: Yes, Ma'm?

MRS. DONNER: Something is needed here . . .

MINERS: Yes, Ma'm!

MRS. DONNER: Such a sad and lonely town,
With only lonely men needs me!

MINERS: Yes, Ma'm!

MRS. DONNER: Well, come on, you weavers of legend,
Make me bold and fancy-dancin' now;
Dress me fine, and call me "Julia!"

MINERS: Julia!

She becomes JULIA BULETTE.

JULIA: And I'll be Queen of the Comstock.
Brave, legendary Julia Bulette
Will set the west on sweet, sweet fire!

MEN: Fire, sweet sweet fire!

WEAVER MEN: When Julia Bulette came into town,
Everybody settled down!

WEAVER WOMAN: Settle down!

MINERS: She brought a bevy of dance hall ladies,
And dressed 'em all in silk and satin,
And bought a brand new white piano,
And played the latest ragtime melodies!

DANCE HALL GIRLS: Saturday night, round a quarter past ten,
That's where you'll find

Virginia City men!
Everybody's steppin' light,
Round Sportin' Row!

JULIA: Y'all come down to Julia's Palace, now!

MINERS: Julia Bulette, turn the lights up bright!
Virginia City ladies are dancin' tonight.
And everybody's feelin' fine,
Feelin' fine 'round Sportin' Row!

MATRONS: Can that extravaganza be
What all the fussing's for?
That so called big bonanza
Behind that bolted door:
For fools, and nothing more!

MATRON #1. I swear, the men have all gone crazy. Yesterday, they made her an honorary member of the fire department.

MATRON #2. Yes, well tomorrow, they're naming a railroad car after her.

MATRON #1. Well, that is the limit!

Continue as written, substituting "There ain't no dames with names like Kitty" *for the final line.*

www.ingramcontent.com/pod-product-compliance
Lightning Source LLC
Chambersburg PA
CBHW072015060426
42446CB00043B/2552